Published by Purnell Books
Berkshire House, Queen Street, Maidenhead

Designed and produced by Grisewood & Dempsey Ltd
Elsley House, 24–30 Great Titchfield Street, London W1P 7SE

© Grisewood & Dempsey Limited 1978

SBN 361 04175 6

Printed in Italy by New Interlitho, Milan

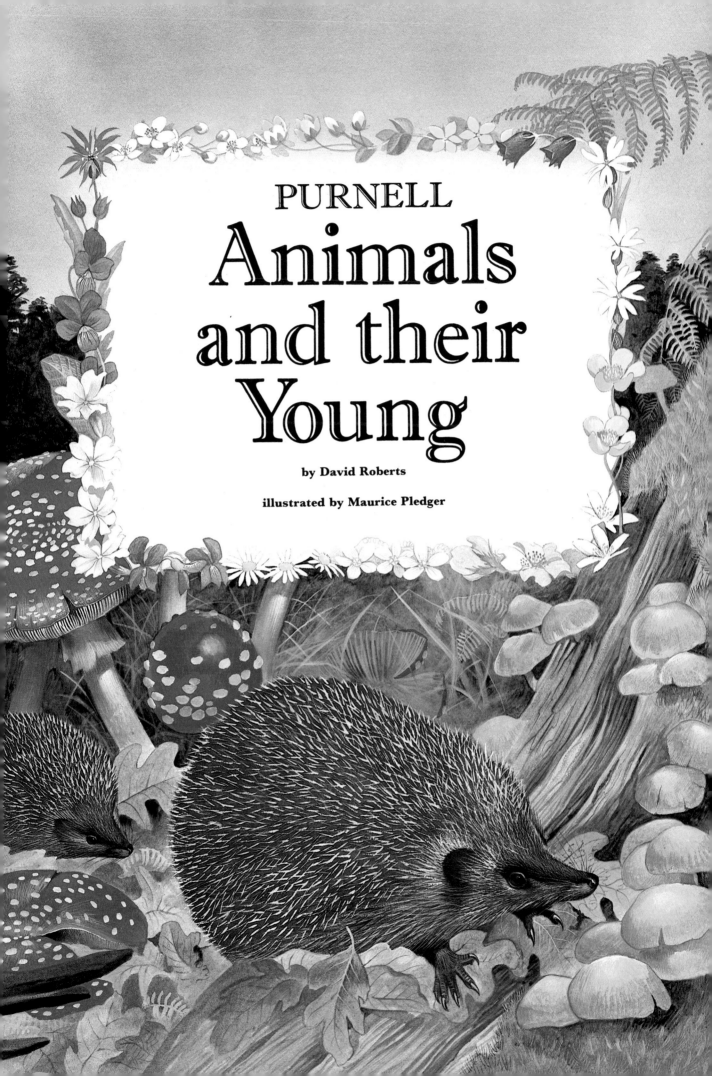

PURNELL
Animals and their Young

by David Roberts

illustrated by Maurice Pledger

Babies who help themselves to mother's milk

ANIMALS whose first food is their mothers' milk are called mammals. When we were babies, we could get our first food from our mothers' breasts, so we are mammals, too.

Mammals with hoofs can usually stand and walk soon after birth. This baby horse, called a foal, can follow its mother, the mare, wherever she grazes to suck the milk from her teats.

Mares usually have foals in springtime when the grass is new and lush. The mare turns some of the grass she eats into milk for her foal.

Here are some more hoofed mammals. The lambs' mother is called a ewe. The donkey foal's mother is a jenny. The nanny goat has a baby kid, and the sow a litter of six piglets. Of course, all these babies have fathers. To have babies, a mare must mate with a stallion, a ewe with a ram, a jenny with a jack, a nanny with a billy goat and a sow with a boar.

Very active babies like these, able to walk about and help themselves to their mothers' milk soon after birth, will try other things to eat as well. They will nibble at grass or food in a trough. When they are eating the same as their parents and have given up mother's milk altogether, they are said to be weaned. Then they are well on the way to being grown up.

The life story of the white admiral

BUTTERFLIES mate tailtip to tailtip. A few hours later, the female is ready to lay her eggs. She finds a honeysuckle, the only plant on which her caterpillars can feed, and lays a single egg on each of the newest leaves.

The mother abandons the eggs to hatch themselves. As the summer flowers fade, the supply of nectar on which she feeds will gradually disappear, and she will die.

Meanwhile, her eggs will have hatched. The tiny larva first eats its eggshell and then begins on its leaf, chewing away from the edge inwards. Between meals, it rests on a bed of silk it has spun in the middle of the leaf. Twice, the caterpillar will get so fat that it will burst its skin. There will be another looser, folded skin underneath.

As autumn comes and the leaves begin to fade, the stem of our caterpillar's leaf must be fastened firmly to the stem of the plant. Then its uneaten remains are wrapped around the caterpillar, the edges fastened with silk. In this cosy, waterproof nest, it will spend the winter.

After six months, it emerges and begins to feed again on the new spring leaves. Twice more, it bursts out of its skin. Now, it is very much bigger and has hairy spikes growing along its back. At last, it uses silk to attach itself to a stem by its hindlegs. It hangs there, its outside turning stiff and crinkly as it changes into a chrysalis. In two weeks, the fully-formed white admiral butterfly will emerge, ready to mate in its turn.

This has been the story of just one butterfly, the white admiral. For others, the details may differ.

How tadpoles leave the water to live on the land

A

B

WHAT is going on in this pond? Look at the pictures A to E above, showing stage by stage how frogspawn becomes tiny frogs. Even better, collect some spawn and watch what happens.

The male frog clings to the female's back, hugging her. As she lays her eggs, he fertilizes them. The frogspawn swells up and floats to the surface. Tadpoles start to form inside the eggs (A).

When the tadpoles first hatch out, they feed on the jelly of their own eggs. They breathe through gills like fish (B).

As they grow bigger, they start to feed on the tiny plants and creatures living on the water weed in their pond. Many of them fall victim to hungry enemies, such as this water beetle (C).

First, back legs grow, as tails and bodies grow bigger (D).

The front legs are growing under the skin. Long after the back legs, the front legs begin to appear (E).

Finally, the tail and body start to shrink, and lungs develop. The baby frog is ready to leave the water. In a day or two, its tail has disappeared. It looks like a tiny version of its parents.

The forest families come out to play

IT is night, and the badgers are about. They have slept all day in their maze of tunnels called a set. Now, the cubs have a friendly scrap before breakfast, just for practice.

The sow has had a busy two months, keeping the nursery clean, suckling her babies and then weaning them on to more solid food by chewing it for them first. Now, they must learn to dig for their own beetles and earthworms, to crack their own snail-shells or partridge eggs, even to catch mice or small rabbits. Perhaps tonight they will find a wild bees' nest and enjoy their favourite treat of honey-coated larvae.

In another part of the forest, a mother fox has brought her cubs out to play. Her nursery, in a special burrow or earth, is lined with fur from her own body. It is out-of-bounds to the dog fox, though he brings the vixen food while she suckles her young. This brood is old enough to venture out.

They, too, have been introduced to solid food. Now, they must learn to hunt for their own. They will begin with worms, insects, frogs, woodmice, even shellfish if they are near a sea-shore. Later, they will learn to chase hares and rabbits, pheasants and partridges, perhaps how to raid a chicken run.

Badgers will fatten up for winter and sleep a lot when it comes. Foxes hunt all year round, tireless in the chase.

Mothers who carry babies about in their pockets

MOTHERS like these belong to a group of mammals called marsupials. The best-known marsupial is the Australian kangaroo. When a kangaroo is about to give birth, she first cleans out her pouch, then lies on her side. The new-born baby looks very little like a kangaroo. It is barely two centimetres long, with front legs slightly longer than back legs. It is quite blind and has not yet grown its ears. It takes about three minutes to crawl into its mother's pouch, where it clings to a teat and begins to suck milk from it. There it stays for six or seven months.

The growing baby rides everywhere in its mother's pouch until it is big enough to stand. At last, it starts to make longer and longer trips on foot. At the first sign of danger, however, it dives head first back into the pouch, turning a quick somersault inside to poke out its head again. Eventually, the mother has to turn it out, when it grows too big or when another new baby is growing in there.

The Australian koala bear is another marsupial. This mother's pouch opens backwards. The tiny, ill-formed baby takes six months to grow large enough to leave the pouch and ride on its mother's back, sharing her meals of eucalyptus leaves. Almost fully-grown youngsters will still hitch a ride.

Some families who live in the frozen wastes . . .

THE Arctic Ocean, bounded by the northern coasts of Canada, Europe and Asia, is always frozen in the area round the North Pole. Its shores, where polar bears live, thaw in the summer.

Polar bears lead lonely lives. Pairs stay together only a few days during the April mating season. Females spend all summer hunting, to put on fat. Not till September do their fertilized eggs begin to develop into new lives. Then the female digs a cave in the snow. As winter approaches, she creeps inside, and falling snow covers the entrance. In this secret nursery, one or two, sometimes three tiny cubs are born.

They remain there four months or more, the mother losing half her weight feeding her babies. In March or April, she brings them out to learn to swim and hunt seals, their favourite food. She will leave them at eighteen months, still barely half grown, to set out upon their lonely lives.

ANTARCTICA is mostly ice-covered land around the South Pole. The emperor penguin breeds on its shores. One egg is laid in May in the winter darkness. The male warms it, holding if off the ice between his toes and a fold of skin on his belly, to hatch it.

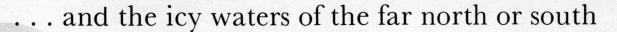

FUR seals belong to the sea lion family who all have small ears. True seals have no visible ears, just tiny ear holes. Fur seals bound over land on all four flippers. True seals use front flippers to drag themselves along on shore, all four for swimming.

Fur seals live in the north and south Pacific and south Atlantic Oceans, mostly at sea, coming ashore to mate and have their pups. In the north, each bull has up to fifty cows; in the south usually only four or five. They mate when the pups from the previous year's mating are about a week old. Cows must leave their pups to take to the sea and feed. The pups lie wrapped in their flippers to keep warm, or wander the beach. On return, the cows pick out their own pups by their cries and smell. A cow's rich milk soon makes up the weight a pup loses while she is away. At three months, it joins its mother to feed at sea.

The female returns from feeding in the sea to feed the chick, while the hungry male goes in search of his first meal for two months. Both parents then take turns in the rearing of the chick. In December, it is ready to go to sea where most of its life will now be spent.

Animals of the African grasslands

MORE than a third of Africa is tropical grassland called savanna, home of the huge grazing herds and animals who prey on them. King of the hunters is the lion.

Lions live in groups or prides of up to thirty, each with its own hunting area. Cubs are born in hiding, away from the pride. While the mother hunts, they are in great danger from other hunters like hyenas. Less than half survive babyhood.

At ten weeks, they are welcomed lovingly into the pride where other lionesses may help to suckle them. As they grow older, the pride can continue its long hunting trips. Cubs learn the art slowly. First kills may be stolen by older companions. Males are often driven from the pride at an early age. Then, they must become kings in their own right.

Ostriches are the watchdogs of the savanna. They are wary birds, taking snatches of sleep of only a quarter of an hour at a time. Their great height allows them to spot approaching danger in the far distance. Other animals, like antelope, graze near them, relying on them to raise the alarm.

The cock mates with three or four hens. Each hen lays ten to twelve eggs, so there may be as many as four dozen in the rough nest on the ground. Both sexes take turns to shade the eggs from the sun with their wings. All the newly-hatched chicks arrive at about the same time. As soon as they have dried out, they can run with their parents. Ostriches cannot fly, but they are among the fastest of all animals on land.

Ostriches, the biggest of all birds, lay the biggest eggs. Yet, compared with the size of their parents ostrich chicks are very small. Elephants, too, heaviest of all land animals, have very small babies. They go on growing to the end of their lives. A 50-year-old bull can weigh over six tonnes. African bush elephants are bigger than their relatives of the tropical forest, and cows never grow as big as bulls.

Elephant cows are among the most caring of mothers. They will suckle their young for up to six years and keep them with them long after they are weaned. Often, they will feed other cows' babies. Such a powerful animal is a delight to watch, gently tending her young.

Proud parents on a sunny spring day in the park

DUCKS, geese and swans all belong to the same family of water birds. They are often found together in large numbers since they like each other's company. They swim on the surface, feeding on the plants and small creatures they can reach by ducking their heads underwater. Swans, with long necks, can feed deeper than the mallards, also in the picture.

Both also feed on land, and there they must go to find a dry place to lay their eggs. Both nest on the ground, usually close to water, though mallards may go some distance before finding a suitable hiding place. Mallards often cover their nests before leaving them to look for food. Swans, both the male cob and the female pen, rely on their size and ferocity to keep enemies away.

Mallards and swans are protective parents. It is a proud day when a mallard duck leads her brood to the water for their first swim, or when a pen gives her cygnets a piggyback ride between her great folded wings.

The salmon's long way home

SALMON are seawater fish. They swim up freshwater rivers only to spawn. The female lays thousands of eggs in a nest called a redd, a hollow scooped out of gravel in shallow, fast-flowing water. She lays the eggs in batches. The males then spread their milt over the eggs to fertilize them. Between 90 and 120 days later, the eggs hatch. The tiny fishes that hatch out are called alevins. They are only about two to three centimetres long. Yolk sacs attached to their undersides supply them with enough food for about 50 days.

When the yolk sac has all gone, the young fish is called a parr. During the next two years or so, it grows slowly into a silvery smolt which is ready for its first visit to the ocean. There it grows rapidly, travelling thousands of miles across the seas. Maybe at the end of that same year or maybe not until some years later, it will find its way back to the river of its birth. How it finds its way, nobody knows. Called a grilse at this stage, the salmon's object is to reach those shallow headwaters that are its spawning grounds. Battling against fierce currents, leaping every obstacle, the salmon fiercely fights its way upstream. Thin, torn and tired, it reaches the headwaters and spawns. Then it drifts away, perhaps to die.

A race for life that few can win

GREEN turtles swim thousands of kilometres across the sea in search of food. Yet, every year, they return to the same tropical beach to breed.

After mating in the shallows, the female must drag her almost half-a-tonne of weight ashore. Here, she has none of the grace or speed shown in the water. She is slow and clumsy, sighing and groaning loudly, and pausing often to rest.

Under cover of night, she scrapes a hollow above the tideline with her front flippers, big enough to hold her whole body. With her rear flippers, she digs a deeper hole into which about a hundred eggs are laid and covered with sand.

Before dragging herself laboriously back to the sea, she disturbs the sand to hide the exact position of her nest. In one breeding season, she will make perhaps four or five of these egg-laying trips.

With the laying and concealment of her eggs, the female green turtle has finished with motherhood. She will probably never see her young. Their hatching and struggle to the sea is their own affair—and a terrible time they have of it.

Many eggs will never hatch at all. Nests will be plundered by jaguars, raccoons, wild dogs, lizards, even men. Successful hatchlings, no bigger than the hollow of your hand, dig their way to the surface, waiting for the cool of the night before breaking through to start their run for the ocean. Even at night, there is a glow of light over the water to guide them.

By that same light, snakes, lizards, crabs and the night heron can hunt them. As dawn breaks, gulls and fork-tailed frigate birds join in the massacre. At sea, the sharks wait. Perhaps from a hundred eggs, one or two adults will grow. It is enough for the species to survive.

The last surviving relatives of the dinosaurs

CROCODILIANS are the only survivors from a large class of prehistoric reptiles called the Archosauria. It included the dinosaurs that ruled the Earth for 150 million years. Alligators get their name from the Spanish *el lagarto*, meaning the lizard. They differ from the true crocodiles by hiding all their teeth when their jaws are shut. Crocodiles expose the fourth teeth on the bottom jaws.

There are two species of alligators, the Chinese one and the American shown here. This is the larger of the two, growing up to five and a half metres long. It mixes mud and rotting vegetation, piling it into a mound as much as a metre high. In this, the female lays a clutch of several dozen eggs.

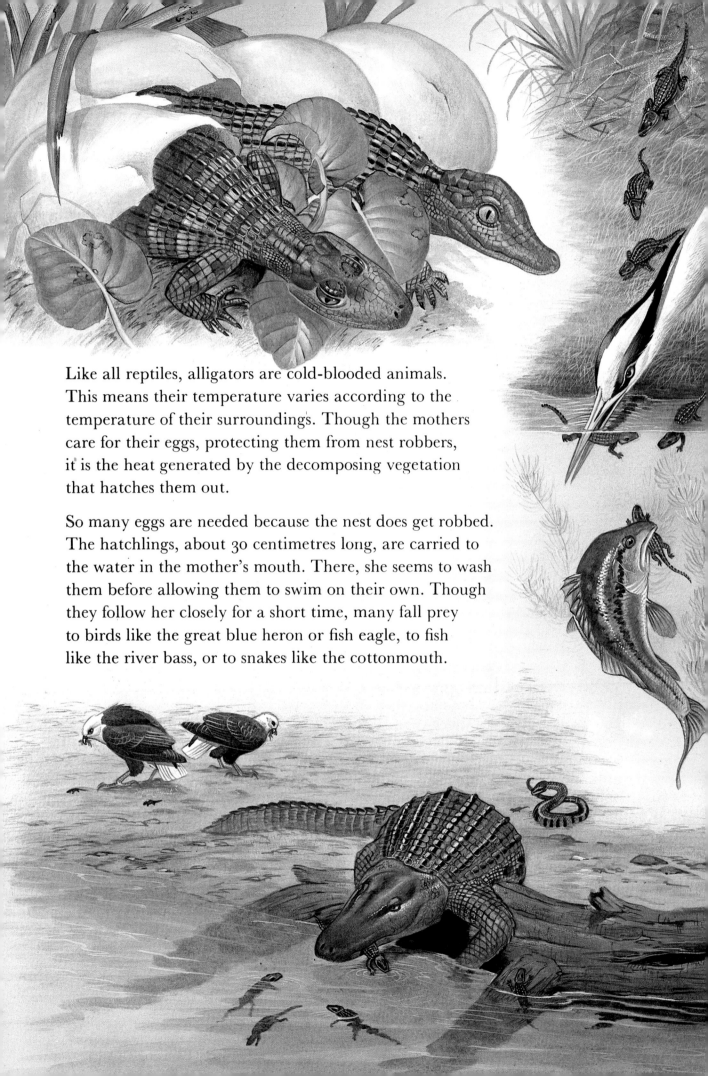

Like all reptiles, alligators are cold-blooded animals.
This means their temperature varies according to the
temperature of their surroundings. Though the mothers
care for their eggs, protecting them from nest robbers,
it is the heat generated by the decomposing vegetation
that hatches them out.

So many eggs are needed because the nest does get robbed.
The hatchlings, about 30 centimetres long, are carried to
the water in the mother's mouth. There, she seems to wash
them before allowing them to swim on their own. Though
they follow her closely for a short time, many fall prey
to birds like the great blue heron or fish eagle, to fish
like the river bass, or to snakes like the cottonmouth.

A busy springtime for the chaffinch family

THE budding hawthorn bush is draped in climbing ivy. Among its shiny leaves, the hen chaffinch builds her nest. The cock watches with interest, but offers her no help. The hen is the builder in the chaffinch family.

And what a marvel her nest is! Moss, lichen, wool, feather or hair is teased out piece by piece to be tucked into place. As the nest grows, she turns round and round in it to form a perfect bowl which will exactly fit her body. Now she is ready to lay her eggs.

Last year, there were six. This year, just four brand-new lives grow inside their shells, in a warm felt bed kept even warmer by a living eiderdown of the mother's body. Only now and then does she

leave to snatch a meal of last year's seeds. The
cock, noisy with song, flits from one corner to
the other of the garden he has marked out, claiming
it for the private use of his own family.

As one by one the eggs crack open, each naked
chick, all gaping mouth, sets up its impatient
chirping. Both cock and hen are needed now to
feed each of those four bottomless begging bowls.
Fortunately, there are plenty of insects. The
chicks swell with food and fluffing feathers.
Appetites grow, and the parents' paces quicken.
As May brings out the hawthorn blossom, the four
chicks overflow the nest. One by one, they hop
out, wings a-flutter to steady their balance.

From a neighbouring bush, the proud parents sing
their encouragement. At last, the boldest chick
lets go its grip, drops, flails its wings—and
lifts itself by sheer courage to another perch.
Where one of them has flown, the rest of those
brave nestlings cannot be far behind . . .

How some mothers cope with their babies

EVERY mother has problems bringing up her baby. The blue whale, for example, is a mammal that lives in the sea but has to breathe air. A new-born baby whale often needs to be carried to the surface to take its first breath. Once its lungs are full, it is buoyant enough to swim by itself. The mother usually needs another female whale to act as 'auntie' and help lift the baby. There are other mothers with transport problems. See here how some of them solve their problems.

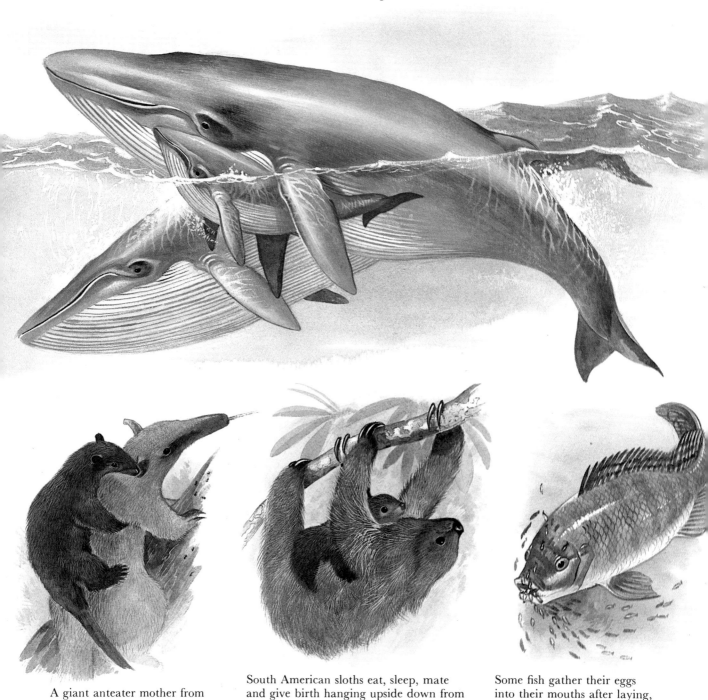

A giant anteater mother from South America, always on the move in a never-ending search for food, carries her single baby everywhere on her back.

South American sloths eat, sleep, mate and give birth hanging upside down from the branches of trees in tropical forests. This mother two-toed sloth makes a fine cradle for her baby who can at any rate begin its life the right way up.

Some fish gather their eggs into their mouths after laying, and hatch them there. Egyptian mouth breeder mothers keep their hatchlings in their mouths until the babies are ready to swim away.

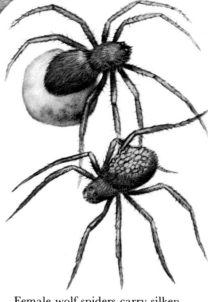

Tiger cubs are often in great danger while the parents are away hunting. So their mothers sometimes carry them to safer hiding places.

The flying fox, a fruit-eating bat and biggest of all bats, sleeps all day and feeds at night. The baby clings to its mother both at rest and in flight.

Female wolf spiders carry silken cocoons of eggs, almost as big as themselves. When the eggs hatch, the spider carries the spiderlings on her back until they can feed themselves.

Sea otters live and breed about a kilometre from the shore they rarely visit. Nursing mothers float on their backs to suckle their young.

As the Surinam toad lays her eggs, the male fertilizes them and sticks them to her back. Her soft skin hardens into pockets where the eggs stay and the tadpoles grow until they turn into little toads.

A chimpanzee mother and her baby have the same close contact as humans do. Until the baby learns to walk, its mother carries it everywhere.

The opossum has litters of up to twenty-five young. Many die while still in her pouch. The ones that survive cling round her when she goes out foraging.

Scorpions are born live, wrapped in a skin which they cut with their stings. For their first seven days or so, they ride on mother's back, feeding on the insects and spiders she kills for them.

Marsupial mothers, such as this wallaby, have the best solution to the transport problem. Even after the joey is able to walk, he can hop back into the pouch for a ride.